New England Memoirs

Nicholas "Nikos" Macenas

PublishAmerica

Baltimore

First printing

ISBN: 1-4137-8231-0
PUBLISHED BY PUBLISHAMERICA, LLLP
www.publishamerica.com
Baltimore

Printed in the United States of America

Dedication

To my wife Denise for continued intellectual support.

To my son Erik for computer genius and outstanding sketches.

To my son Mark for beautiful sketches.

A Country Store — New England's Best

The atmosphere is homey,
friendly and very North country
People sitting around a potbelly stove
chatting and talking about the fierce storm raging outside
Old and young contributing to the discussion
It is warm and cozy in these surroundings
Fun and talk now end because the storm has taken a turn
and become a blizzard

Country store gathering
Outside the storm intensifies,
You know New England weather
Storm is fierce with high winds
Snow drifts accumulate
We are quite warm and cozy
Together we continue to have our discussion
Forgetting what is happening out of doors
Now we rise, not believing our eyes
Almost buried beyond escape
Shovels at hand, out we go
Scoop after scoop, tunneling to our vehicles
We're out and homeward bound finally
We all had an endless conversation
Interrupted by Mother Nature
The end of a memorable gathering at the country store

A Fall Walk

Dream to walk on a fall morning, breath leaves you in a cold mist
Be aware of the beauty around and under foot
Travel down the path, view the spectacular natural panorama with every step taken
Listen carefully of the forest sounds
From all directions see birds hover over
Squirrels, chipmunks scurry along the dew covered ground
Deer grazing in a field nearby
Leaves cascading down as if over a waterfall
Sit on a stone wall and look up at the brilliant clear blue sky
Affix your eyes on the gorgeous Vermont landscape
A picture of sculptured beauty

A Winter Poem

A winter of white, a glistening array of icicles hanging on a shack
Deep, deep the snow that falls on the fields of hay
Cattle huddled to fend off the cold winter wind
Children scurry to and fro, frolicking in the snow
Build a snowman as big as you can
Make him smile so more snow will fall
Pastures covered with the new crystals of white
Church steeples glisten as if glassed over
Sun later bears down leaving pallets of shiny, glistening mirrors
on the newly fallen snow
Roadways not yet plowed seem never trodden on by any living thing
Automobiles covered with white and barely visible
Deer hidden in a grove of trees, warm and secure
Cold whistling wind gnawing at our cheeks
Walk and trudge along a path of newly fallen snow
Happy to be able to see and enjoy winter's wonder
Love it, believe, heavenly grace is ours to keep.

Antique Door

Pass through this door of antiquity
The facade old and withdrawn
Famous may have entered here
Look at its stone walls
Built of hand-hem slate
Design as old as Jefferson himself
Assemble Colonials all to talk
Men ready to fight for freedom
Liberty for our citizens
Lincoln proclaims slaves no more
Enact laws for calm not to be
Civil war begins amiss
Brothers part company
A brutal battle campaign
The battle end has come
Truce and settle sides
To quell the anger
Rejoice, rejoice, it's calm again
A peaceful, peaceful mind

Apple Cider, Apple Pie

Sweet with tang
Golden brown with spice
Crisp the taste
From brightly colored red
Or maybe green
Delicious and scrumptious
Crunch crunch
My, oh my, a healthy treat
From the tree
Grow apple grow
The season short
And pick we will
I love them so
Apple, apple, be mine
Apple pie for me
Apple crisp for you
Apple anything for all
It is the fruit of life
Healthy we all will be

Charming Friend

Conversation undaunted
From the start
Years pass
Manage professionalism without effort
Kindness exemplified
Brain power full of thoughtful expression
Tutoring for the youthful mind
A sincere smile always present
A positive approach
A daily pleasing attitude
Forget not a breath of refreshing air
That you are

Country Barbecue

Peaceful evening, the night sky bright with starlight
Friends at fireside beam with smiles of delight
The glow of all faces in the amber light
Toast the happy faces with a cup of cheer
A night of contentment for all here tonight
Sit and dream of nothing but happy thoughts
Friendly country people knowing true fellowship
To feast, feel pleasure of the night
Stars brilliant in the sky, fire flies aglow
Warmth of the fire, shadows tall abound
All around us the crisp cool of night
The end of a blissful evening
Good night
Farewell for now, my friends
See all soon again

Fluttering Heart

A journey to the unknown
Calm facial expressions comfort the heart
Sensitive it is, longing for undying, unconditional faith
Fuel the fire of love, devotion
The vantage point is feelings
How interwoven is a healthy heart
The heart must explode profound joy
To live and react to love
Pride in the heart provides filtering with time
Temptation connects the strings
That respond to thoughts of affectionate pursuit
Take stock, repress anger and frustration
Intimacy propagates love with the heart
Its weight minimal, its habits quick to respond
To retrieve silent affection

Friends

Fun with best of friends
Laughter and great treats
Linger in warmth of the hearth
Play games, piece puzzles
Retire, good night of slumber
Peaceful, sweet dreams
Arise, aroma sumptuous breakfast
Outside romp in the snow
Afternoon nap to calm the senses
Dine, roast prime ribs of beef
Dessert brighten meal to end
Time well spent and companions kept
Prepare to trek home
Remember next trip to come

Friendship Is

Meet and acquaint with one
Amazement the twain does combine
A gift to give, return not required
Fulfill a thirst for companionship
A jewel that shines so bright
The reflection bounces to so many
Flex and bend for every ounce of friendship
Those who give eventually receive
Live life, happiness is friendship
A heart feels comforted
Quench your thirst for thee
Through a monocle a view
Small or large, a rainbow explodes
Forth and forever
Friend, friend, an acquaintance will be

Graceful Forest

Forest of green, maples of brown, birch of white, hemlocks of red
Floor of moss mingle with earth that covers the ground
Peer at the sky of azure blue
How intense the clouds are that pass so quickly
Change the glance to move from treetop to treetop
At a limb, birds of the forest fly so fast from one to another
The ground teams with movement of squirrels, mountain hare, raccoon
The field mice scurry here and there hunting for a meal
Up in the sky an eagle soars over the forest floor as graceful as can be
In the distance a family of white tail deer, how entrancing the joy of wild life
As far as the eye can see, view the land everlasting, be compassionate
Reinforce and protect our environment for future generations
Reflect, enjoy, protect, the future is ours for all eternity

Hand in Hand with Laughter

Clasp the hand ever so gently
Signify a sign of friendship
Conjure and extend a smile
Extend that happy feeling onto those
Who have none to give
All the while continue to perpetuate a grin
Be guilty, offer a smile
As a grin begets a smile
A grin creates a chain reaction
Stomach wrenching pain and tears stream down
So laughter erupts for those who create one
Amazing quotes enhance, communicate laughter
Live, grin, smile, laugh
Lighten up
For seriousness disappears and a sense of humor explodes as vulcanic rumblings
Humor is hidden in everyday life
Laughter is a natural sense
Laud over laughter
Humor is deep in the soul
Climb that pinnacle of humor
The seed of happiness is physical cleansing
Smiling and laughing people live long, healthy lives
The feeling may be close to insanity, so share a smile
Lighten up for sure
And soon

Red Clover

Red clover, red clover, three leafed over
To bees the nectar of life
Honey made from clover
Sweet the taste of honey
Breezes blowing here and there
Clover color thy fields with red
Sun reflecting gleam of red
Speckles of red and green
Admire the vast fields of clover
Natural to the Vermont landscape

Hawk

A bird in flight
Wings of speed
Soar up, up and away
Beam your prey below
Hawk I think must be
Beautiful God of the skies
Round and round to circle
Down and down to drop
Catch that meal for all
Talons sharp to grasp
Return to nest of young
Eat, my pretties, eat
Grow to leave the nest
For now you're grown
Soar up, up and away

Lake

On the shore, gentle waves ripple
Look across the lake
Hear the sounds of the night
Dusk has come
Loons sing the song of the night
Clouds, deep, dark and gray, ominous they are
Across the mountain range
A mist falls on the lake like a cloak
From the peaks above, the wind whips across the treetops
Ghosts of the forest say, "Sway trees in the cold breezes of the night."
Winter chill will soon appear
The lake will soon be covered with a blanket of ice
Frozen, frozen so cold
Winter bright and clear
Stay silent, listen, listen
The sound of crystals of white falling
Reflecting as minute mirrors gleaming on the floor of the land
Be dazzled by the wonders of nature

The place, Morgan, Vermont, about 10 miles from the Canadian bounder, winter of 1999. We travel from New Hampshire, for approximately four and a half hours. We reach this country home of our friends. Location is on the shore of Lake Seymour in the section of Vermont referred to as the Northeast Kingdom. The majestic picture of the lake is captivating, with the distant view of the mountains in the background. In the distance, hear the sounds of the loons in song and fish jumping out of the water making circular pools and rippling effects on the water's surface; the sight is mesmerizing.

Lake Seymour

Be ever so graceful the sprawling lake
Sun shines on the surface with gleaming images
Distance is far in the horizon as the eye can see
Surrounded on all sides by mountains majestic
The day dims, suddenly the sun lowers behind the mountain cliffs
The sun has gone for now, to return tomorrow
Evening mist covers the lake like a blanket of fog
Night falls into silence, and the sound of the loons resound in the night shadows
Signaling that night has come
The lake sleeps
Another wonderful, sunny day will come

Lilies on the Pond

From the depth of the bottom
Intermingle the strands of lilies
Tentacles extend to the surface
A flower of white emerges
Bringing vibrant color
A pond in spring is populated throughout
Skim the water with the eye
Green pods lay aimless and serene
Absorbing sunlight rays
spread lily petals, white
sun so high, warm and bright
the pond water stirs, a sunfish jumps from beneath
an insect snatched to nourish itself
a ring of rings remains
calmness of the lilies return
standing on the pond's edge
birds in the trees sing their melodious song of spring
Rhythms mingle with cool breezes and the warmth of the sun
Perhaps a painter's dream
But at last it is not
listen to the world of the pond with a keen sense of hearing
See the glimmer of pools, the surface
always responsive to natural reality

Mount Monadnock Trek

Clouds resemble soldiers in formation
Winds racing across ragged cliffs
Sun reflecting off of stone expanses
From the mountain peak focus on clusters of ponds and lakes below.

The trail begins at a tree line of evergreens, hardwoods
Nearing the peak growth becomes scarce and rock faces begin their prominence
Within rock faces, water filters through
Many trails to the peak
Trails dotted with hikers young and old
Suddenly startled by a glider hovering and soaring overhead
Wings straight as an arrow
Away it disappears into the distance
At the summit, rocks are jagged, weathered by seasons of inclement weather
On the way up and down the mountain, within crevices spout wild, bright,
vibrant pink lustrous blooms
At about the halfway point something caught my eye
Fossilized impressions of large bird claws
Chipmunks and red squirrels scurrying about the cliff faces
At the summit, carved into stone, names of hikers from years past and present
On the descent, rocky ledges turn into green, lush forest and the base of the
mountain is a carpet of green
A plethora of ponds and angular lakes become more prominent
Distant cities on this clear, crisp day are evident north, south, east, and west
Mount Washington and the Presidential Range in view
Plants, low and tall, nature's fan of beauty
The landscape portrays itself
an abstract puzzle connecting at its start and its end.

Loons

Morning mist on lake so calm
Sound of melody so faint
Sound so vocal heard afar
Oh, so stately handsome bird
Skim the surface of the lake
Along will follow family so close
Focus loons to feed
Down they dive to feast
Later up to rise
Alas a morsel for to nourish
The morning past and noon has come
Loons glide on and on
Young follow along
Leaving a wake behind
Soon evening will come
The haunting sound of the loon to peak
Sound filters through the cool night air
The sound so pure
Nature's drama unfolds again
Resounding melody for all to hear
Night falls into darkness
Another day to come

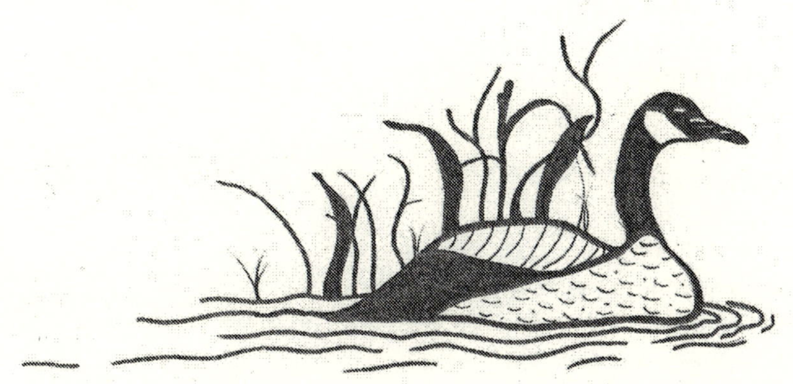

Hermit Thrush

Flight from south
Wings of flight to north
Light on branches high
Nest on branches low
Hide in waving, flowing plumes of grass
Swoop to pond below
Drink of water fill
Wind ripples on water's flow
Over waterfall it goes
Breezes pass fondly by
Sun is bright
Clouds sentinels of the skies
Hermit Thrush flutter thy wings
Stay for a season short
Away, fly south again
Soon to see you next season again.

Mountain Cog Rails Up

Winter's cold, chilling winds
Tracks commence below
Winding, entwined above
Leads to mountain green
Peak of green shadowed by sparse, ghostly clouds
Sun peers through it all
Brace for a trip to the top
Train on track
Around the base a haunting whistle blows
Echoes throughout the valley low
Clouds disperse, resounding light explodes
Green trees in multitude, alas
Pine, birch, maple, beech, all in tune, rock faces telescope throughout the white mountains
The sound of breezes whisking through and through
Skeletal rock formations in mass
A view of wide and wonderful earth
A string mountain peaks, astonishing sight
Return; smoke billowing from the steam engine as old, as not really known
Down we travel after a tour up top
Pictures taken of the wonders captured, eternal
Finally a picture of green, spring and summer, a final thing
As sun sets in the east, so do the clouds filter the sun's rays!
Day becomes twilight, then darkness of night
Fall colors next, then winter alas begins
White mountain trip complete.

MOUNT
WASHINGTON
COG RY.
AMMONOOSUC
WASHINGTON
RAILWAY
COMPANY
1866

Mountain Fragrances

Shimmering leaves of color glow
Bond together, create a flow
Delicate fragrances of yore
Tantalize our sense of swell
Nature's clover seen afar
Fields of grasses swaying in the wind
Mountain crest, a sight to behold
From tree to tree a bird will light
Mingle all the mountain lore
The honeybee to pollinate
The flowers combine a delicate find
Mountain fragrances grand and fair
To all enjoy its grandeur

Natural Color Feast

Fall feast leaves, to winter chill
Fall, the season of colorful fantasy with the
season in mass
Feel the cool breezes on your cheeks
remark how wonderful the sun shines
Pumpkin plenty, corn stacks bent
As they remember springtime
Fall ends soon, winter's chill upon us
Soon, amazing droplets of moisture will come
Creating the white of snow

Spring Is Maple Sugar Season in Vermont

In past decades, the collection of maple sap went like this.

Old-fashioned Mornings

The work began with a big country breakfast, men eating and chatting about the process of gathering sap, and the tasks designated during the work day. A sugar house on the property, just a short walk on a dirt road from the farm house, was where every spring the sap from the maple trees was collected and boiled down to what some still call "the nectar of the forest."

The weather for maple sugaring must be cold at night and fairly warm during the day to allow the sap to run into the tapping buckets. In past decades, gathering this sap from the trees was arduous and demanding. Buckets would have been connected to taps and hung on the trees to collect the sap drippings. The following day, collection would begin by emptying all the sap into a large vat carried on a wagon-drawn by two large draft horses or oxen.

After collection, the liquid would eventually be brought to the sugar house for the boiling down process. It is a dream to relish and remember.

Modern Workdays

The current way of collecting sap today is generally done by the use of a pipeline. The pipeline is plastic tubing that is attached to each tree and allows for the sap to simultaneously flow into the stainless steel vats.

After the sap is collected and brought back to the "sugar shack," it is poured into a large metal unit where the boiling down process begins. The unit is known as an evaporator. An evaporator is constantly being fed firewood to keep the liquid at a hot temperature for the boiling process.

Indulge Your Taste Buds

It takes 40 gallons of sap to produce one gallon of syrup. The end result after all this hard work: 100% organic, pure maple syrup in grades of A and B, dark and amber, an entire assortment of enticing tastes.

Use this natural flavoring on pancakes, cereals, oatmeal, and ice cream—as a substitute for sugar. Be inventive, try it as a glaze on ham or pork. Maple syrup can be a special treat for children of all ages. To indulge in a special snack, take a portion of the syrup and drop onto fresh clean snow. Watch the syrup crystallize and become a sweet, snowy delectable treat.

The Tradition Continues

Maple trees are found only in the northeastern states and Canada. There is an annual Vermont Maple Festival every year. To learn more about the fantastic tradition of syrup making, come join us! It is a pleasant experience—I guarantee it.

Nectar of the Forest

In the spring breezes
Trees are waving—
Night cold and crisp,
The days warm.
As the sap runs
The sugar shack is ready,
Gasping plumes of steam,
Gobbling the sap to make nectar—
From within comes an
Unbeatable taste

Ode to Green Mountains

Spring leaves flutter
Red clover in fields alive
Sail along, monarch butterflies
Pollinate, sweet honeybee
Cattle roam fields of clover
Perky are bunches of dandelions
Spring is here, sap cometh
Maple syrup will flow
Summer fun coming soon
Fun time, swim, hike, and travel
Around the corner fall will be
Autumn here, fall leaves tumble
Kaleidoscope of colors seen
Beyond winter, freezing cold
Winter crisp and clean
White wonderland of crystals of snow
Ode to green mountains

Rain, Gentle Rain

Simple, cool mist emerging from moisture laden clouds
Trickling gentle droplets that nourish the earth
Scramble between raindrops
Lifting the spirits
How mysterious this thing, rain
Sound so rich with song
Sing praise of nature's melody
Spring rain beads on blades of grass
Moisture collects on leaves of trees
Bow limbs with sweetness of gentle rain
Suddenly, elusive clouds part
Sunshine peers through funnels of divine light
Beams warmth
Sweet goodness
Conjure a smile

Quechee Gorge

Rippled water, oh so far
Down continue to the sea
Meandering over stone and falls
Sparkling rolling river, go
Pictures snapped from far above
Mountains high from side to side
Autumn colors vivid, so
Take a walk to gorge below
Long bridge above so high
Sugar maples abound nearby
Picturesque Vermont to be
Ever all for us to see

Spot on Down East Map

Rain comes in sheets of moisture
Inlet tide is out
Wind blows, ripples on the surface
Water skirts along the tributary
The eyes see, ears hear
Natural, remarkable scene
Coastline, seaweed visible
As tide enters in force
Suddenly clouds explode
A pelting torrent of rain ensues
Rain wavering, east to west
Calmness sauntering in and quickly as it came, it disappears
Lightning pounds the coast
Shoreline trees glisten with droplets of dew
Growth drinking moisture for life
Protruding stones at low tide
Showing are limbs on bottom's silt
An ocean cormorant appears
Swooping for fish delight
Plunging, submerged eternal
Up it soars to the surface
A tasteful morsel in beak
At a dock a canoe waves aimlessly on a tidal pool
Maine wind churning the current
Tiny waves moving helter skelter, to and fro
Gulls glide on the ocean tide
Their flight a photo to the eye
Calls to each other fill the ocean air
Breezes concoct a musical tune in the cove
On the roof of the island cottage rain marks time, so constant

Bullets of rain peacefully drop onto the rooftop
A blessing of earth's tender grace
The ocean breezes spear as rain hovers over the inlet cove
A storm has come in as a lion and moves out like a lamb
"Behold we are, DOWN EAST.
"MAINE THAT IS."

Peaceful Birches

To be in the grace of beauty
Behold the tender birches as they sway in the wind
It is a balmy day in the picturesque Vermont countryside
The sight will elevate the senses
Flowing colors on the trees, as the leaves shimmer with every telltale whisper
of the wind
Be still, look at the clear blue sky
The birch leaves and the clear blue sky create an artist's canvas
In the pasture see stacks of hay standing tall
Children dancing around them and ready to jump on them
A multitude of trees, azure blue sky, and children playing
Combination of all delight in this picture of fun
The birches swing to and fro in the wind, bewitched by the whisper of fall to come
Walk the pathway through these gentle sentinels of the forest
Bask in the joy of the azure blue sky with sparse clouds moving slowly by
A mountain range surrounds you from the movement you could make
Memorize the unmistakable, constant changes, as you tread on this country soil
An adventure has begun and ended with a clean breath of invigorating air
Clean, fresh, crisp mountain air—inhale, think, remember, and retain its beauty.

Peaceful Birches

Sunbursts

A kaleidoscope of vibrant color
The horizon folds the rays as far as the eye can see
Gleaming sunlight, birds perched on limbs absorbing soothing warmth
Always solar rhythm conveyed, beguiling fountains of warmth
Rivers, oceans, mountains—accept its need to nourish, protect its continuing
environment
Jewels of the earth
Reflecting beams throughout
Clear, natural air
Life-giving energy
From the mist of sunrise dazzle produce happy moments, clouds distant not seen

Tranquil Past

The road leads to a place in the past
It is the example of peace and tranquility
Be reminded of the pioneers of yesteryear
Emotions abound and dream of a restful time
Love what the eye sees of creation's best
Favor thoughts in total happiness
Truly think clearly of thy sight
Always have faith the earth is Mother Nature
It is ours, a resourceful beauty

Waterfall

Water, water, going where
To pond and lake
Over dam and over falls
To not know where you end
Winter gone
Water flow
Spring has come
Mountain water pure
Fill the lakes and ponds with graceful flow
To drink, to swim
To savor more
Pure water pure

Apple Cider

On a special autumn day
A man named Brad
Pressed apples a tad, so glad
The juice flowed like mad
The golden stream, the buckets hold
A cider press as good as gold
A farmer's hand undaunted with gusto, that's Brad

Children fascinated with every turn of the crank
All impressed, young and old
Rainbow of cider, the color of gold
Pulp pressed, down the juice it flowed
River pure runs nature's mold in gold
Spirits high, sun bright, wind so cold
Leaves in splendid red and gold
Fall harvest of apples as winter nears
Drink a cup of autumn cheer

Silent Darkness

Silent darkness is emitted
As the sun lowers in the western sky
Trees statuesque as the flaming sphere peers through tall, lumbering trees
Rainbow of colors effect in the evening horizon
Peaceful offering of diminishing light
Fading rays of cherished sunlight
Winter's chill finally over
Metamorphic growth of green
Camouflaging the forest
Sprouts for and seeds of growth
Gloom of winter gone
Spring flowers on the rise
Calm winds radiating sunshine
Capture the atmosphere
A plethora of earthly wealth
Tranquil end to a spectacular day
Plunging the day into darkness
Ultimate sight of vibrant starlight
Sky of the heavens
Explore with the naked eye
Surge with balanced cold seeping from the fields
Shadows in the mist of eve

Gazebo

Turn-of-century history
An octagonal design
Treasured center piece
Peaked copper roof
Fringed, spiraled trellises
Railing configured surround
Hanging flower baskets fragrant
Boxed combinations colorful
Stairway leads onto red brick pathways
Patches variable hues on oval's grove
Gardens of miniature roses pink
Antique lighted post illuminate
Social, cultural, presentations seasonal
Presidential candidates orate
Voices past generations speak
Spring flowers bloom
Promenade oval summer evenings
Summertime, concerts begin
Fall brings autumn, pumpkin fest
Sooo monstrous pumpkins
Contest of weight
Extravagant autumn foliage
Halloween, children's parade, review
Winter sparkles of white
Shivering frosty smiles
Kids all aglow
Kris Kringle arrives
It's Christmastime
Total sense of pride
Our town's heritage

Boulder Loop Trail

Mount Washington within range
Path of trail onto Boulder Loop
We four backpack each
Baby birch tree in one
Soil, fertilizer in two
Water for feed in three
Lunch for us in four
Off to trek the trail
Rocks jutting along the way
Tree stumps protruding up
Steep the climb
Stop rest, take a breather
Brambles impend progress
Stones resemble faces
Strenuous the way
At the top
Heart pounding view
What an experience
Panoramic shot magnanimous
Father's request
Legacy
Plant this tree

Picture of Lilacs

Mountain hill background
Bud in early spring
Minute white flowers sprout
Sunshine brilliant, flowers turn
Become clusters of small droplets
Mesmerizing scent complete
Limbs connect sprays of lavender mingle
Grove of purple beauty scattered
Imagine lilac powdery rare
Picture New England eastern native
Lilac, lilac pleasing seasonal fare

Ocean Shores

Distant getty protects the shore
Isles of Shoals binocular shown
Sea gulls circle tide pools in
Wind cold , whistling off water vast
Beach sands cloud the air, weeds tumble
Chill of winter, bitter, sky clear
Hilly, lichen-covered dunes
Winding path, sea shore's edge
Waves small reaching in
Sand pipers scurry along
Lighthouse signals ships at sea
Foghorn distress a sound calls
Winter tide retracts at sunset
Night falls on ocean beach
Evening sky valiant blue
Winter solstice, Alies, Cancer, Libra, Capricorn
A splendid nighttime show

Young Moose

Young moose foraging grass
Field of waving green
Wind whistling through the trees
Forest shadowed by lumbering masts
Baby looks up, sees us
Frightened it is not
Closer and closer we get
Inquisitive this mammal
An apple in hand
Try to feed it
Anticipating a charge
Drop fruit to the ground
Afraid we are too close
We back away
It eyes us with concern
Comes ever so near
Apple gone
Pictures taken, a fond memory
Wonderful encounter

Covered Bridges

Patriarchs of old North
Rooted through generations
Constructed of native pine
Monument of history
Level, quality-built, solid
Original works by craftsman
Of a bygone era
Great old Yankee ingenuity
Fragile, practical, weathered
Inspirational view unique
Turn of the century built
Remnants, days past
Of historic annals
Image through portal of time
Dinosaur of bygone days
Pictorial scenes initiated as art
Buggy ride to church
Stolen kisses under bridge
Fishing seated at stone's edge
Drop wreath to water, Memorial Day
Haunting remembrances
Horses, oxen cross daily
Withstand harsh winters
Picture summer's gentle rain
Spring sunshine emits its rays
Autumn colors heavenly
Remain still, New England forever

Apple Orchard

Winding country road
Leads to soldierly rows of trees
Blossoms pink and white
Grass carpet of green
Wild flowers throughout
Tree trunks angled abstract
Above thousands of blooms
It is springtime
From blossoms to fruit
Almost an instant visual phenomenon
Festival of red, it's fall
Apples, apples a horde
Ladders up, ready pick
Hand a basket fill to brim
Away to home, dear people eat
Cook and bake at will
An adventure, el naturale

An Untold Story of Vermont

A place in the past, a farm on a hill top… This allows a view of the fields that were once cultivated and planted with wheat and alfalfa that fed the cattle that grazed and roamed the vast expanse that covered acres and acres of pastures. The house sits on a plateau as a scene out of a Norman Rockwell painting. A magnificent home with many rooms and a kitchen with old-fashioned values that allowed the family to prepare food the good old-fashioned way. Wood burning cast-iron stove and a beehive hearth for baking bread, wonderful cakes, cookies and pies… The smell I can remember so well.

A barn with stacks of hay gathered in the fall for the cattle to feed on during the winter months… The winter conditions were very, very cold, and it lasted for a long, blustery and blizzard time. There were staircases in all parts of this house to climb to the upper floors and to the pantry that was situated on the second floor. The staircases were spiraled and very narrow to climb. The ceilings were low to allow the heat from the oilfired furnace to rise to all levels of this history laden edifice.

Tractors and baling machines were at the ready to do their work in the fields of plenty. Life was hard but very rewarding to the family that lived for generations on this farm.

Field of dreams to those who dare live a farming life
A life of the plentiful harvest and the abundance without strife
The sight of cattle in the fields, chickens cackling in the barnyard
A farmer's delight at being called to lunch by the sound of the bell at the kitchen door
Lunch over, back to work, get that field plowed for planting, it's spring.
Winter is finally over, wild flowers beginning to bloom
Apple trees well pruned in the fall of last year now show their blossoms
Spring brings the sap to make maple syrup for pancakes and whatever
Summer is time for fun but the work in the fields and home must continue on
Summer has about now left the farm, and we have harvested the hay, picked the apples, prepared all of the preserved foods for the oncoming winter

The fall foliage is a spectacular sight while winter's cold is very near
Splendor are the vast fields on the hill
Old, a farm house with history untold
Generations of history could totally never be told
Life and happiness of hard work toiled
Fashioned by folks from an old mold
A road of ages truly and endlessly untold
Life hard and rewarding to those who are bold
Tender are their lives with values that hold
Forever is the seed of mind and soul
The heart of those in the fields of earthly soil
Those have the endless joy of believing their work was done
Slumber with restful night for a new day will begin.

Snow Machine

We go onto the farm of an ancestral property, another home of our family friends. The very special activity that remains in my mind, is the one snowy day during the winter of… I'm not sure of the year. A snowmobile ride in the forest, around the house with my son, was, to say the least, an experience not ever to be forgotten. My son and I started our trek into the woods adjacent to the farm on an excited note. The ride began out very smooth, until the snow machine decided to stall.

We were in very dense woods, and also, I could not start the snowmobile. I stayed as calm as I possibly could, trying to figure out a solution. It was starting to get dark, and I was getting a bit nervous. We did not wish to be stranded in these woods throughout the night.

Luck was about to appear. My Vermont friend decided that we were out too long, and came out to rescue us from our ordeal. He reached under the hood and pulled a lever, and the machine started to purr. My son and I mounted the snow machine and proceeded to barrel through the snow at a fast pace. We finally came back to the comfort of the farm and to the happy faces of all our family members.

Nostalgic Reunion

Lunch Car Dining

The neon sign out front reads "Louis' Diner"
Bright red with silver trim
Expect the best
Think 1940's, homemade, delicious food
Open for business WOW! From 8 a.m. to 8 p.m. daily
Jukebox playing upbeat tunes
Counter stools and booths packed with hungry folks
Need conversation and a cup of jo
Come here
Spill your troubles
We will listen
Passing through town, stop in
A bright, cozy happening in New Hampshire's capital city, Concord
Always a smile and an endless pot of coffee
Waitresses bellowing food orders to chefs Paul and Alex
Responding fast to customer satisfaction
Time does not stand still
The year is 1982
Louis', as we've known it, closes its doors
Gone but not forgotten
Louis' is hauled away
Restoration
A museum reopened to its former glory in Rhode Island
A centerpiece of American history
We loved and adored Louis' Diner
Of course Louis was the "man"

Babbling Brook

Oh, babbling brook cool
Crystal clear water
Forward eddy to pool
Directionally flows abstract
Low branches restrict its way
Ripples, gurgles, on its onward course
Zigzagging lazily upon the forest floor
Wisp of wind whistling through the forest canopy
Birds sing on trees above
Stream of endless charm
Gentle breezes, a smell of spring
A breath of fresh air
Sun funnels mirrors of reflections
Gathering cumulus clouds darken
Rain bursts down, pelting the brook
Storm ends
Multicolor rainbow tranquil in the sky
Sky, clear blue as a bell
Babbling brook onward
Casually, down, down, down

Granite Hideaway

We are on a trip to the top of a mountain crest, to a granite hideaway, which has been described as having ghostly inhabitants. Begin the drive to the top of the world, obviously in your imagination. You're on a winding road that bends to and fro up to this monstrous stone structure that is quite an incredible sight.

A stone edifice that rises to the clouds in view of the green mountains of Vermont at every turn of your head… Focus on the vast beauty that is an inspiration to see. The fall foliage beams with unparalleled brilliant colors. Upon entering the home, we see an enormous fieldstone hearth that reaches to a vaulted ceiling, unimaginable that anything as this could be built. A spiral staircase of polished brass and wrought iron leads to a sanctuary with cavernous windows overlooking the amazing Vermont landscape. The gardens of fragrant, colorful flowers and plush lawns have a look of green moss. Stonewalls encompass the entire compound, which also boasts an apple orchard and sugar maple trees standing as soldiers in formation. Sit in the gazebo and gaze at the heavenly wonders of our great land. Relish the sights and sounds of the elusive forest. Notice the different trees and spectacular array of wild flowers and berries that thrive in the woods. Bend; pick blueberries and blackberries. Clusters of mushrooms are everywhere. Ghosts of past lives are said to have roamed the confines of this enormous house. The residence is said to have been a home of a Union Civil War general. He was wounded in a battle and returned home. It is told that his family still roam these halls. A passage leads from the luxurious outside gardens underground into a dug dirt cellar that enters into the house. Ghostly footsteps are heard moving throughout. The feeling was eerie; a flash of light appears as if the general's apparition is there. The image is and appears to be the soldier that past on many years ago.

The Elusive Ghostly Dream Place

The elusive dream place may be imaginary, and in spirit or reality
The all reaching mind tells all that exist, but who really knows for sure
The mind is a super way to dream of beauty at its best
We have the sense to believe that it is ours to enjoy
Continue, yes, to not forget that we need to protect all for generations to come
Dispute not, that it all could be lost to decay; do not be amiss to that possibility
The place in the clouds if only in my imagination and love the scene
Earth is sensitive and vulnerable and could be destroyed without care
Believe in Mother Earth for its internal and external joy.

Old Man

'Tis said that he exists eternal
Expression powerful, silent
A gracious, protective gift, life-like
Scope of vision, mountain vigilant
Sharp, keen, sensitive features
Poetic warrior everlasting
Creation universal, a work of art
Engraved view, safeguarding
All-encompassing mountains
Its sculptured profile, mystical
An apron, bodice of green
Years of wear, disaster strikes
Lead to final rest
A great loss for human kind
Never a photo again

Love True

To those who know not true love
Connect to one who exudes it so
Filter some to your heart
Try not to figure the potion
The eye cannot see
It only falls in place for thee
It is absorbed only for that special one
A life without is wasteful love
Love that one on that path of praise
For no one knows except the one
Who experiences love of life?
A soul mate is true
A life for always and forever

Printed in the United States
32971LVS00005BA/1-81